PYTHON PROGRAMMING FOR STUDENTS

Dr. Firoz Kayum Kajrekar , PhD

Assistant Professor, Dept. of CS & IT
S P K Mahavidyalaya, Under Mumbai University

DEDICATION

TO MY PARENTS
KAYUM & TAHIRABI
For making me to believe that anything was Possible

TO MY WIFE
AFREEN
For making everything Possible

TO MY CHILDREN
SARA & SAFA
For making things Possible

CONTENTS

ACKNOWLEDGMENTS

Python is a programming language that is used for general purposes. It is described as a high-level programming scripting language but may also be put to use for non-scripting contexts. It embraces code readability and the ability to express programming language using only a few lines of codes. Python intents to create clearer programs for small programming uses as well as for complex and large scale programming use.

This book will teach you basics of Python as a Programming Language and will also take you through various advance concepts related to programming. It gives you an introduction to programming in Python from the ground up, starting with tips on installation and setting up your programming environment, and moving through the core parts of the Python language in a logical order

The book doesn't assume any previous knowledge, and introduces fundamental programming concepts like variables, loops and functions using simple terms and easy-to-follow examples that you can run and modify.

This book has been prepared for the computer science graduates to help them understand the basic to basic concepts related to Python Programming Language. After completing this book you will find yourself at a moderate level of expertise in using Python for software development, where you can take yourself to next levels.

Before you start proceeding with this tutorial, I'm making an assumption that you are already aware about basic computer software concepts like what is keyboard, mouse, monitor, input, output, primary memory and secondary memory, operating systems and applications etc. If you are not well aware of these concepts then I will suggest going through a short tutorial on Computer Fundamentals.

CHAPTER 1

INTRODUCTION TO PROGRAMMING

1.0 INTRODUCTION TO PROGRAMMING

A program is a set of instructions that tell the computer to do various things; sometimes the instruction it has to perform depends on what happened when it performed a previous instruction. This section gives an overview of the two main ways in which you can give these instructions or "commands" as they are usually called. One way uses an *interpreter*, the other a *compiler*. As human languages are too difficult for a computer to understand in an unambiguous way, commands are usually written in one or other languages specially designed for the purpose.

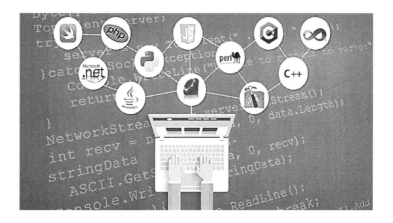

Interpreters

With an interpreter, the language comes as an environment, where you type in commands at a prompt and the environment executes them for you. For more complicated programs, you can type the commands into a file and get the interpreter to load the file and execute the commands in it. If anything goes wrong, many interpreters will drop you into a debugger to help you track down the problem.

The advantage of this is that you can see the results of your commands immediately, and mistakes can be corrected readily. The biggest disadvantage comes when you want to share your programs with someone. They must have the same interpreter, or you must have some way of giving it to them, and they need to understand how to use it. Also users may not appreciate being thrown into a debugger if they press the wrong key! From a performance point of view, interpreters can use up a lot of memory, and generally do not generate code as efficiently as compilers.

In my opinion, interpreted languages are the best way to start if you have not done any programming before. This kind of environment is typically found with languages like Lisp, Smalltalk, Perl and Basic. It could also be argued that the UNIX® shell (sh, csh) is itself an interpreter, and many people do in fact write shell "scripts" to help with various "housekeeping" tasks on their machine. Indeed, part of the original UNIX® philosophy was to provide lots of small utility programs that could be linked together in shell scripts to perform useful tasks.

Popular Interpreters available

Here is a list of interpreters that are available, with a brief discussion of some of the more popular interpreted languages.

BASIC: Short for Beginner's All-purpose Symbolic Instruction Code. Developed in the 1950s for teaching University students to program and provided with every self-respecting personal computer in the 1980s, BASIC has been the first programming language for many programmers. It is also the foundation for Visual Basic.

Lisp: A language that was developed in the late 1950s as an alternative to the "number-crunching" languages that were popular at the time. Instead of being based on numbers, Lisp is based on lists; in fact, the name is short for "List Processing". It is very popular in AI (Artificial Intelligence) circles. Lisp is an extremely powerful and sophisticated language, but can be rather large and unwieldy.

Perl: Very popular with system administrators for writing scripts; also often used on World Wide Web servers for writing CGI scripts.

Scheme: A dialect of Lisp that is rather more compact and cleaner than Common Lisp. Popular in Universities as it is simple enough to teach to undergraduates as a first language, while it has a high enough level of abstraction to be used in research work.

Icon: Icon is a high-level language with extensive facilities for processing strings and structures.

Logo: Logo is a language that is easy to learn, and has been used as an introductory programming language in various courses. It is an excellent tool to work with when teaching programming to smaller age groups, as it makes creation of elaborate geometric shapes an easy task.

Python: Python is an Object-Oriented, interpreted language. Its advocates argue that it is one of the best languages to start programming with, since it is relatively easy to start with, but is not limited in comparison to other popular interpreted languages that are used for the development of large, complex applications (Perl and Tcl are two other languages that are popular for such tasks).

Ruby: Ruby is an interpreter, pure object-oriented programming language. It has become widely popular because of its easy to understand syntax, flexibility when writing code, and the ability to easily develop and maintain large, complex programs.

Tcl and Tk: Tcl is an embeddable, interpreted language, that has become widely used and became popular mostly because of its portability to many platforms. It can be used both for quickly writing small, prototype applications, or (when combined with Tk, a GUI toolkit) fully-fledged, featureful programs.

Compilers

Compilers are rather different. First of all, you write your code in a file or files using an editor. You then run the compiler and see if it accepts your program. If it did not compile, grit your teeth and go back to the editor; if it did compile and gave you a program, you can run it either at a shell command prompt or in a debugger to see if it works properly.

Obviously, this is not quite as direct as using an interpreter. However it allows you to do a lot of things which are very difficult or even impossible with an interpreter, such as writing code which interacts closely with the operating system or even writing your own operating system! It is also useful if you need to write very efficient code, as the compiler can take its time and optimize the code, which would not be acceptable in an interpreter. Moreover, distributing a program written for a compiler is usually more straightforward than one written for an interpreter—you can just give them a copy of the executable, assuming they have the same operating system as you.

As the edit-compile-run-debug cycle is rather tedious when using separate programs, many commercial compiler makers have produced Integrated Development Environments (IDEs for short).

1.1 REASON WHY PYTHON IS GOOD

Are you an aspiring programmer who is stuck on which programming language to start with? It's probably a tough choice, especially if you want to learn programming to build a career. Very understandably you want your choice of programming language to be the right one. Many learners begin by asking around and end up even more confused because different people will suggest different languages, each one informed from their own experiences. Some people will suggest Java or .NET because they are enterprise languages. Yet others might suggest JavaScript because it is gaining ubiquity across the stack, while some may suggest Ruby or Python.

While each camp may have valid reasons for their choice, I personally suggest Python to everyone who is stuck with the question of which language of begin with. My rationale is simple - start with a language which allows you to learn programming without wrestling with an unreasonable amount of paraphernalia to distract you from your main task. Not only does Python achieve this aim very well, but it also has a great job market.

Also remember that your first programming language is not your last one. It's a starting point from where you will learn many more languages. We have long gone past the era where developers could code their entire career in one language. But Python is a great first language. Following are explanation why we can learn python as our first programming language:

Easy to set up and get started

Software development has become a bit of a beast nowadays. There's just way too much a person has to install and understand before they can write their first line of code. This is very frustrating for someone who is just starting because it distracts them from what they really should be focusing on - which is to learn the principles of programming.

Python really shines in solving this problem. It's super simple to get started with Python because of its simple setup. Python also has a straight forward syntax which will not drown you with complex constructs, once again allowing you to focus on principles of programming without getting frustrated with ancillary concepts like directory structures and the like.

Even though I am a big fan of object oriented programming, I like the fact that Python allows you to get started without learning about classes and objects. OOPs is very important because Object Oriented is a slightly complex concept which should ideally be taught after more basic concepts of programming are grasped well. Python will allow you to get started with simple things really fast and also work on complex concepts after you have grasped the more basic ones.

Extensive standard library and third party tools

The standard library is the library of classes and modules which come along with the language as part of its core capabilities. It's important to have a substantial standard library because it allows developers to do standard stuff without having to hunt for third party code which can be a pain and unstable as well.

However, when a newbie does proceed beyond basic knowledge they will need to work with third party libraries and Python shines out here too. It's hard to believe that something you need has not already been implemented as an open source library by someone from the community.

One of Python's most-touted strengths is its standard library, and for good reason. It comes with over 400 modules, ranging from a minimal HTTP server to databases, to compression libraries.

Helpful community

In my personal experience Python has one of the most helpful communities out there. Flame wars happen everywhere, but they happen the least in the Python community, so as a newbie you will never be apprehensive of asking questions. This is important because I have seen places where newbie questions are often met with disapproval and even indignation. This silly sort of arrogance is a very unhealthy attitude that has unfortunately crept into the software industry. Fortunately you won't have to deal with it as a Python developer. Even if you do run into such episodes, they will be far and wide. Python also has a lot of user groups and meet ups. Chances are that your city or town already has a Python user group. Such groups allow newbies to interact with senior developers for learning as well as for exploring work opportunities.

Great job market

At the beginning I mentioned that your first programming language should be one which will help you learn the principles of programming and not necessarily a language that will land you the juiciest job. However, with Python it's not an either-or situation. Python has a thriving job market and is used extensively for web development and scientific computing.

According to the Tiobe index, Python has moved up from the 7th most popular programming language in November 2014 to the 5th in November 2015. And the Redmonk index for June 2015 ranks Python at #4. So chances are that you will land a very good and satisfying job with Python.

The Zen of Python

If you are not already convinced then the Zen of Python will make you a believer for good...

- Beautiful is better than ugly.

- Explicit is better than implicit.

- Simple is better than complex.

- Complex is better than complicated.

- Flat is better than nested.

- Sparse is better than dense.
- Readability counts.
- Special cases aren't special enough to break the rules.
- Although practicality beats purity.
- Errors should never pass silently.
- Unless explicitly silenced.
- In the face of ambiguity, refuse the temptation to guess.
- There should be one preferably only one --obvious way to do it.
- Although that way may not be obvious at first unless you're Dutch.
- Now is better than never.
- Although never is often better than *right* now.
- If the implementation is hard to explain, it's a bad idea.
- If the implementation is easy to explain, it may be a good idea.
- Namespaces are one honking great idea -- let's do more of those!

1.2 INTRODUCTION TO PYTHON PROGRAMMING LANGUAGE

Python is an example of a high level language.Other high level languages you might have heard of are C++, PHP, Pascal, C# and Java. Python is an easy to learn, powerful programming language. It has efficient high-level data structures and a simple but effective approach to object-oriented programming.

History of Python

Python is a fairly old language created by Guido Van Rossum. The design began in the late 1980s and was first released in February 1991.

Why Python was created?

In late 1980s, Guido Van Rossum was working on the Amoeba distributed operating system group. He wanted to use an interpreted language like ABC (ABC has simple easy-to-understand syntax) that could access the Amoeba system calls. So, he decided to create a language that was extensible. This led to design of a new language which was later named Python.

Why the name Python?

No. It wasn't named after a dangerous snake. Rossum was fan of a comedy series from late seventies. The name "Python" was adopted from the same series "Monty Python's Flying Circus".

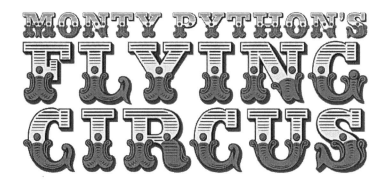

Release Dates of Different Versions

VERSION	RELEASE DATA
Python 1.0 (First standard release)	January 1994
Python 1.6 (Last minor version)	September 5, 2000
Python 2.0 (Introduced list comprehensions)	October 16, 2000
Python 2.7 (Last minor version)	July 3, 2010
Python 3.0 (Emphasis on removing duplicative constructs and module)	December 3, 2008
Python 3.5 (Last updated version)	September 13, 2015

1.4 FEATURES OF PYTHON PROGRAMMING

Simple

Python is a simple and minimalistic language. Reading a good Python program feels almost like reading English, although very strict English! This pseudo-code nature of Python is one of its greatest strengths. It allows you to concentrate on the solution to the problem rather than the language itself.

Easy to Learn

As you will see, Python is extremely easy to get started with. Python has an extraordinarily simple syntax, as already mentioned.

Comparing the code to be written in C language, python coding is very simple and easy.

```cpp
1 #include stdout
2
3 int main()
4 {
5     std::cout << "Hello, world!\n";
6 }
```

And here's code with the same output in Python 3:

```python
1 print("Hello, world!")
```

Free and Open Source

Python is an example of a FLOSS (Free/LibrÃ© and Open Source Software). In simple terms, you can freely distribute copies of this software, read it's source code, make changes to it, use pieces of it in new free programs, and that you know you can do these things. FLOSS is based on the concept of a community which shares knowledge. This is one of the reasons why Python is so good - it has been created and is constantly improved by a community who just want to see a better Python.

High-level Language

When you write programs in Python, you never need to bother about the low-level details such as managing the memory used by your program, etc.

Portable

Due to its open-source nature, Python has been ported (i.e. changed to make it work on) to many platforms. All your Python programs can work on any of these platforms without requiring any changes at all if you are careful enough to avoid any system-dependent features.

You can use Python on Linux, Windows, FreeBSD, Macintosh, Solaris, OS/2, Amiga, AROS, AS/400, BeOS, OS/390, z/OS, Palm OS, QNX, VMS, Psion, Acorn RISC OS, VxWorks, PlayStation, Sharp Zaurus, Windows CE and even PocketPC !

Interpreted

A program written in a compiled language like C or C++ is converted from the source language i.e. C or C++ into a language that is spoken by your computer (binary code i.e. 0s and 1s) using a compiler with various flags and options. When you run the program, the linker/loader software copies the program from hard disk to memory and starts running it.

Python, on the other hand, does not need compilation to binary. You just run the program directly from the source code. Internally, Python converts the source code into an intermediate form called bytecodes and then translates this into the native language of your computer and then runs it. All this, actually, makes using Python much easier since you don't have to worry about compiling the program, making sure that the proper libraries are linked and loaded, etc, etc. This also makes your Python programs much more portable, since you can just copy your Python program onto another computer and it just works!

Object Oriented

Python supports procedure-oriented programming as well as object-oriented programming. In procedure-oriented languages, the program is built around procedures or functions which are nothing but reusable pieces of programs. In object-oriented languages, the program is built around objects which combine data and functionality.

Python has a very powerful but simplistic way of doing OOP, especially when compared to big languages like C++ or Java.

Extensible

If you need a critical piece of code to run very fast or want to have some piece of algorithm not to be open, you can code that part of your program in C or C++ and then use them from your Python program.

Embeddable

You can embed Python within your C/C++ programs to give 'scripting' capabilities for your program's users.

Extensive Libraries

The Python Standard Library is huge indeed. It can help you do various things involving regular expressions, documentation generation, unit testing, threading, databases, web browsers, CGI, ftp, email, XML, XML-RPC, HTML, WAV files, cryptography, GUI (graphical user interfaces), Tk, and other system-dependent stuff. Remember, all this is always available wherever Python is installed. This is called the 'Batteries Included' philosophy of Python.

Besides, the standard library, there are various other high-quality libraries such as wxPython, Twisted, Python Imaging Library and many more.

1.5 APPLICATIONS OF PYTHON

Web Applications

You can create scalable Web Apps using frameworks and CMS (Content Management System) that are built on Python. Some of the popular platforms for creating Web Apps are: Django, Flask, Pyramid, Plone, Django CMS. Sites like Mozilla, Reddit, Instagram and PBS are written in Python.

Scientific and Numeric Computing

There are numerous libraries available in Python for scientific and numeric computing. There are libraries like: SciPy and NumPy that are used in general purpose computing. And, there are specific libraries like: EarthPy for earth science, AstroPy for Astronomy and so on. Also, the language is heavily used in machine learning, data mining and deep learning.

Creating software Prototypes

Python is slow compared to compiled languages like C++ and Java. It might not be a good choice if resources are limited and efficiency is a must.

However, Python is a great language for creating prototypes. For example: You can use Pygame (library for creating games) to create your game's prototype first. If you like the prototype, you can use language like C++ to create the actual game.

Good Language to Teach Programming

Python is used by many companies to teach programming to kids and newbies. It is a good language with a lot of features and capabilities. Yet, it's one of the easiest languages to learn because of its simple easy-to-use syntax.

CHAPTER 2

PYTHON INSTALLATION

2.0 PYTHON DOWNLOAD AND INSTALLATION INSTRUCTIONS

The Python download requires about 30 Mb of disk space; keep it on your machine, in case you need to re-install Python. When installed, Python requires about an additional 90 Mb of disk space.

1. Click https://www.python.org/downloads/ The following page will appear in your browser.

2. Click the Download Python 3.6.2 button. The file named python - 3.6.2.exe should start downloading into your standard download folder. This file is about 30 Mb so it might take a while to download fully if you are on a slow internet connection. The file should appear as

3. Move this file to a more permanent location, so that you can install Python (and reinstall it easily later, if necessary).

4. Feel free to explore this webpage further; if you want to just continue the installation, you can terminate the tab browsing this webpage.

5. Start the Installing instructions directly below.

a. Double-click the icon labeling the file python-3.6.2.exe. An Open File - Security Warning pop-up window will appear.

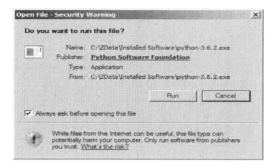

b. Click Run. A Python 3.6.2 (32-bit) Setup pop-up window will appear.

Ensure that the Install launcher for all users (recommended) and the Add Python 3.6 to PATH checkboxes at the bottom are checked. If the Python Installer finds an earlier version of Python installed on your computer, the Install Now message will instead appear as Upgrade Now (and the checkboxes will not appear).

c. Highlight the Install Now (or Upgrade Now) message, and then click it. A User Account Conrol pop-up window will appear, posing the question Do you want the allow the following program to make changes to this computer?

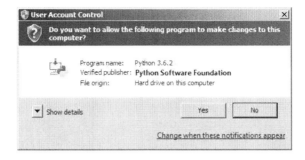

d. Click the Yes button. A new Python 3.6.2 (32-bit) Setup pop-up window will appear with a Setup Progress message and a progress bar.

During installation, it will show the various components it is installing and move the progress bar towards completion. Soon, a new Python 3.6.2 (32-bit) Setup pop-up window will appear with a Setup was successfully message.

e. Click the CLOSE button and python should be installed by now.

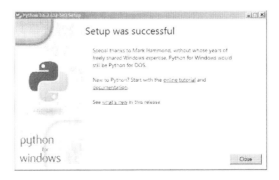

2.1 INSTALL PYTHON

Installing Python is generally easy. Nowadays many Linux and UNIX distributions include a recent Python. Even some Windows computers notably those from HP now come with Python already installed. If you do need to install Python, you can download from Python official website.

The engine that translates and runs Python is called the Python Interpreter. There are two ways to use it:

1. Immediate mode

2. Script mode

1. Immediate mode

In this mode, you type Python expressions into the Python Interpreter window, and the interpreter immediately shows the results.

For example:

>>>2+2   #User input

4   # The interpreter responds with this

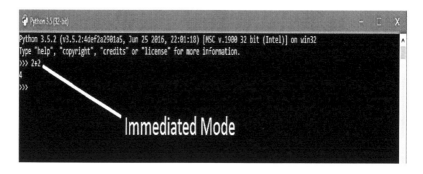

The >>> is called the Python prompt. The interpreter uses the prompt to indicate that it is ready for instructions. We type 2+2, and the interpreter evaluated our expression, and replied 4, and on next line it gave a new prompt, indicating that it is ready for more input.

2. Script mode

Alternatively, you can write a program in a file and use the interpreter to execute the contents of the file. Such a file is called a script.

2.2 INSTALL PYTHON ON YOUR WORKSTATION OR LAPTOP

Python is free to install. You can install it from the Python web site. Note that we will use Python 3.x, and not the older 2.x releases. because it matches the textbook. See below for an explanation of program release number.

Install Python from the Python web site

1. From a browser go to: http://www.python.org/

2. On the left, under Quick Links (3.x.x, the x may change with Python updates) click the Windows Installer link

3. A popup window appears asking whether you want to save the python-3.x.x.msi file, click Save File

4. Select a folder on your workstation to save it

5. Go to that folder, and click on the file (python-3.x.x.msi)

6. Take the defaults at each step (click Next)

7. When installation is complete, click Finish

Python will now be among your installed programs: To start the IDLE IDE, click start --> All Programs >> Python 3.x --> IDLE (Python GUI).

Operating Python IDLE

The current version of Python is Python 3.2. The first thing we'd like to do is actually start running the Python program development tool named IDLE, which should be listed in installed programs under Python tab.

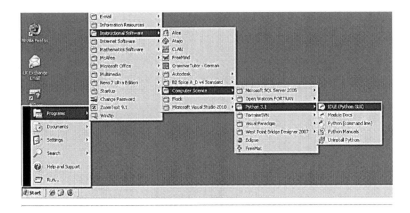

A new window will open up as shown in following figure.

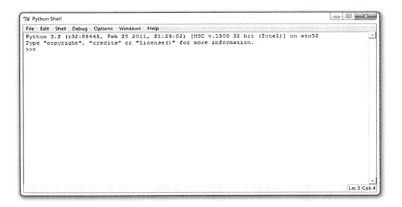

This is the main window to IDLE, and what we see right now is called the Interpreter or shell window. The Interpreter allows us to enter commands directly into Python, and as soon as we enter in a command, Python will execute it and display its result. We'll be using this Interpreter window a lot when we're exploring Python: it's very nice because we get back our results immediately. If it helps, we can think of it as a very powerful calculator.

As per tradition, let's get Python to say the immortal words, "Hello World".

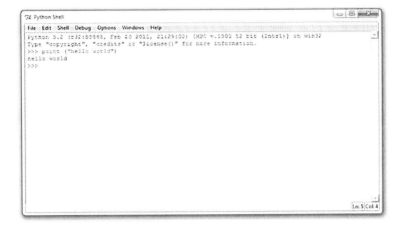

Those '>>>' signs act as a prompt for us: Python is ready to read in a new command by giving us that visual cue. Also, we notice that as we enter in commands, Python will give us its output immediately.

Let us see some more examples as follows

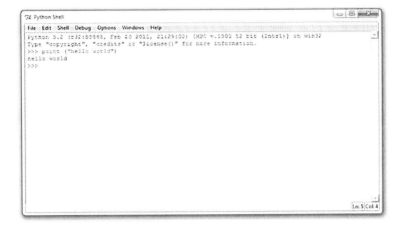

Note that the "print i," line is indented. This is a Python rule for the "for" statement that will be covered later. Don't worry too much about knowing the exact rules for making programs yet: the idea is that we can experiment with Python by typing in commands. If things don't work, then we can correct the mistake, and try it again.

2.4 HOW TO SAVE THE FILE IN PYTHON IDLE

If we close down Python and start it up again, how do we get the computer to remember what we typed?

The solution is a little subtle: we can't directly save what's on the interpreter window, because it will include both our commands and the system's responses. What we'd like is to make a prepared file, with just our own commands, and to be able to save that file as a document. We can later open that file and "run" Python over it, saving us the time of retyping the whole thing over again. For example, let us open a new window

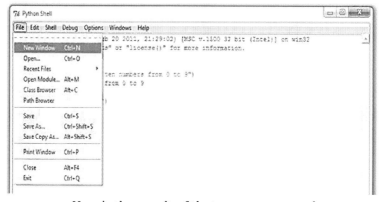

Here's the result of that menu command:

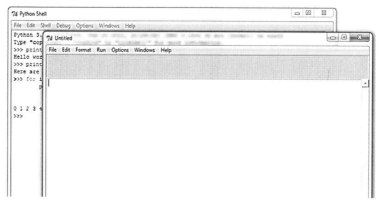

We notice that there's nothing in this new window. What this means is that this file is purely for our commands: Python won't interject with its own responses as we enter the program, that is, not until we tell it to. I'll call this the *Program window,* to distinguish it from the *Interpreter window.*

What we wanted to do before was save our program that we had tried out on the interpreter window. Let's do that by typing (or copy/pasting) those commands into our Program window. You can copy/paste by highlighting (hold the right mouse button down while you move the mouse over the text to be copied) what is to be copied, click on the "Edit" option to the right of the "File" option, click the "Copy" option, then in the Program window, move the cursor to where you want to copy the text, then click "Edit" and "Paste".

Ok, we're done with copying and pasting. One big thing to notice is that we're careful to get rid of the ">>>" prompts because they're not really part of our program. The interpreter uses them just to tell us that we're in the interpreter, but now that we're editing in a separate file, we can remove the artifacts that the interpreter introduces.

Let's save the file now. The Save command is located under the File menu:

When you click "Save" you will be asked where to save the file. To save your programs for access when you leave the lab, save it to a flash drive or to your locker. For example, click "computer", click on the L drive, click on the folder where you want to save the file. Supply a file name for example: yournameLab0.py Don't forget the file extension ".py". If you forget it, it will be more difficult to find the file when you want to reopen it later.

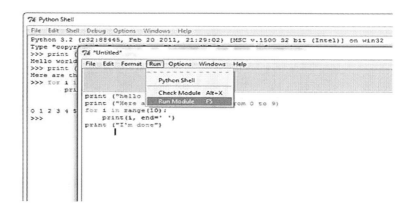

Now that we've saved the program, how do we run the program? If we look at the menus on our program window, we'll see that there's a menu option "Run Module", and that's what we'll do. What we want to see is Python running through the program, and displaying its results in the Interpreter window.

2.5 PYCHARM

PyCharm is an Integrated Development Environment (IDE) used in computer programming, specifically for the Python language. It is developed by the Czech company JetBrains. It provides code analysis, a graphical debugger, an integrated unit tester, integration with version control systems (VCSes), and supports web development with Django. PyCharm is cross-platform, with Windows, macOS and Linux versions. The Community Edition is released under the Apache License,[3] and there is also Professional Edition released under a proprietary license - this has extra features.

To Install PyCharm on a Windows Operating System

1. To get to the installer, first you must make a JetBrains Educational Account. (article.aspx? articleid=18808) (Note: you will have to confirm your account through your email)

2. Go to JetBrains and download the PyCharm
   http://www.jetbrains.com/pycharm/

3. Click the Download button found in the middle of the page or in the top right corner of the screen.

4. After clicking download, the website will ask what platform and whether you wish to download the Professional or Community option. Keep Windows selected and click Professional.

5. After clicking the button, a browser button will appear in the bottom left corner of the screen. When it is done downloading, click the button. If the button does not appear, navigate to your Downloads folder and open the PyCharm setup &le.

6. The Setup Wizard should open up. Click Next to continue.

7. The program will ask for an install location. Click Browse if you wish to change the default location. Click Next to continue.

8. Installation options available are 32-bit launcher and ".py". Keep both unchecked and click Next to continue.

9. Choose a Start Menu Folder. Keep JetBrains selected and click Install.

10. When the program is done installing, click Finish.

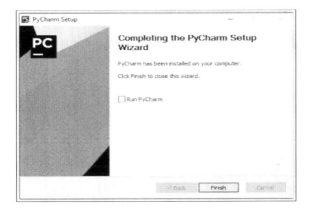

CHAPTER 3

PYTHON EXPRESSION

3.1 THE STRUCTURE OF A PYTHON PROGRAM

A Python program is a sequence of statements. Python executes this sequence of statements in a specific, consistent, and predictable order. A Python statement contains zero or more expressions. A statement typically has a side effect such as printing output, computing a useful value, or changing which statement is executed next. A Python expression describes a computation, or operation, performed on data. For example, the arithmetic expression 2+1 describes the operation of adding 1 to 2. An expression may contain sub-expressions — the expression 2+1 contains the sub-expressions 2 and 1. An expression is some text a programmer writes, and a value is Python's internal representation of a piece of data. Evaluating an expression computes a Python value. This means that the Python expression 2 is different from the value 2. This document uses typewriter font for statements and expressions and sans serif font for values.

3.2 HOW TO EXECUTE A PYTHON PROGRAM

Python executes a program by executing the program's statements one by one until there are no more statements left to execute. In general, Python executes statements from top to bottom.

Python executes a statement by evaluating its expressions to values one by one, then performing some operation on those values. Python evaluates an expression by first evaluating its sub-expressions, then performing an operation on the values. Notice that each sub-expression might have its own sub-sub-expressions, so this process might repeat several times. However, this process of dividing and evaluating always terminates because the expressions become smaller at each step until they reach some base expression.

For example, to evaluate 2*10 + 6/3, Python first evaluates 2*10 to the value 20, then evaluates 6/3 to the value 2, then adds the two to get 22. Note that in order to evaluate one expression, Python evaluates several smaller expressions (such as 2*10). Furthermore, to evaluate 2*10, Python evaluates the expression 2 to the value 2, and so forth. The value of a literal expression such as 2 is the corresponding value, so this is where Python stops dividing into sub-expressions.

3.3 PYTHON EXPRESSION

Literal Expressions

A literal expression evaluates to the value it represents. Here are some examples of literal expressions and the values to which they evaluate:

17 → 17
"this is some text" → "this is some text"
8.125 → 8.125
True → True

This document uses → to show an expression on the left and the value to which it evaluates on the right.

Binary Expressions

A binary expression consists of a binary operator applied to two operand expressions. A binary operator is an operator that takes two arguments for example, + or /.

To evaluate a binary expression to a value, Evaluate the left operand which is an expression to a value and replace that operand expression with that value. Evaluate the right operand which is an expression to a value and replace that operand expression with that value. Apply BIN OP to the two resultant values, obtaining the value of the binary expression. Replace the entire binary expression with this value. In general, a binary expression has the form: ***EXPR BIN OP EXPR***

Here are some examples of binary arithmetic expressions, each of which evaluates to a number.

*2 * 5 → 10*
14 + 8 → 22

Here are some examples of binary Boolean expressions, each of which evaluates to a Boolean - True or False

6 == 7 → False
0 < 5 → True

Some expressions don't evaluate to numbers or Booleans. For instance, applying the + operator to two string values evaluates to the concatenation of the two strings:

Have a + very good day → "Have a very good day"

Compound Expressions

When at least one of the operands is itself an expression for example in 2 * 5 + 1, the expression is a compound expression.

To evaluate a compound expression to a value, use order of operations to identify the main operator the last operator that you'll apply, for example, the main operator in 2 * 5 + 1 is, +, so 2 * 5 + 1 is an additional expression. Identify the operands to the main operator. Then evaluate this expression the main operator and its two operands as you would evaluate a binary expression.

Python follows the standard mathematical order of operations, so 2 * 5 + 1 is equivalent to (2 * 5) + 1. Here are some examples of compound expressions:

> $2 * 5 + 1 \rightarrow 11$
> $2 + 5 - 1 \rightarrow 6$
> $4 * 6 / 8 \rightarrow 3$

You can use parentheses to override Python's order of operations, or just for clarity. A parenthetical expression has the form: *(EXPR)*

A parenthetical expression evaluates to the same value as the enclosed sub expression, EXPR, does. For example, (22) evaluates to the same thing 22 does, namely 22. As another example, 2 * (5 + 1)) 12

Unary Expressions

A unary operator operates on a single value. In general, a unary expression has the form: *UN OP EXPR*

To evaluate a unary expression to a value, evaluate *EXPR* to a value and replace EXPR with that value. Apply *UN OP* to the value and replace the entire expression with the new value.

Two common unary operators are not and -. The not operator negates a Boolean value; for example, not False evaluates to True. Used as a unary operator, the - operator negates a numerical value; for example, - (2 * 5) evaluates to -10.

3.4 PYTHON VARIABLES

Think of a variable as a container. A variable stores a value so that you can reuse it later in your program. This reduces redundancy, improves performance, and makes your code more readable. In order to use a variable, you first store a value in the variable by assigning the variable to this value. Later, you access that variable, which looks up the value you assigned to it. It is an error to access a variable that has not yet been assigned. You can reassign a variable, that is, give it a new value, any number of times.

Note that Python's concept of a variable is different from the mathematical concept of a variable. In math, a variable's value is fixed and determined by a mathematical relation. In Python, a variable is assigned a specific value at a specific point in time, and it can be reassigned to a different value later during a programs execution.

Python stores variables and their values in a structure called a frame. A frame contains a set of bindings. A binding is a relationship between a variable and its value. When a program assigns a variable, Python adds a binding for that variable to the frame or updates its value if the variable already exists. When a program accesses a variable, Python uses the frame to find a binding for that variable.

To evaluate a variable access expression to a value, search the frame for a binding from VAR EXPR to a value. If such a binding exists, replace the access expression with that variable's value. Otherwise raise an error, because the variable is not defined.

Below is an illustration of a Python frame with bindings for 5 variables:

A	→	12
i	→	"sawantwadi is good"
fnum	→	5
s	→	False
J	→	True

Variable access expressions let you use the value of a variable you've assigned. Suppose that the frame is the one illustrated above, where a variable with the name x is assigned the value 13. Then the expression x evaluates to the value 13. Here are some examples of variable access expressions:

answer →42

(answer + 2) / 2 →22

In general, a variable access expression has the form: **VAR EXPR.** For now, *VAR EXPR* is a variable name.

An assignment statement creates a variable and sets its value, or changes the value of an existing variable.

To execute an assignment statement, Evaluate EXPR to a value and replace EXPR with that value. If the variable already exists in the frame, change its binding so that it now refers to the value from the previous step.

Otherwise, create a new variable in the current frame and bind it to the value from the previous step. In general, an assignment statement has the form: **VAR EXPR = EXPR.** Here are some examples of assignments:

x = 18

y = x + 1

*y = y * 2*

CHAPTER 4

CONDITIONS AND LOOPS

Decisions in a program are used when program has conditional choices to execute code block. Let's take an example of traffic lights, where different colors of lights lit up at different situations based on the conditions of the road or any specific rule.

It is the prediction of conditions that occurs while executing a program to specify actions. Multiple expressions get evaluated with an outcome of either TRUE or FALSE. These are logical decisions and Python also provides decision-making statements that to make decisions within a program for an application based on the user requirement. Python provides various types of conditional statements:

4.1 STATEMENT DESCRIPTION

if Statements

It consists of a Boolean expression which results is either TRUE or FALSE followed by one or more statements. Python if Statement Syntax

if expression();
statement;

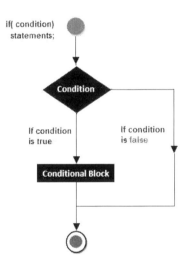

Here, the program evaluates the test expression and will execute statements only if the text expression is True. If the text expression is False, the statements are not executed.

In Python, the body of the if statement is indicated by the indentation. Body starts with an indentation and the first unintended line marks the end. Python interprets non-zero values as True . None and 0 are interpreted as False.

Example:

> *a = 15*
>
> *if a > 10;*
> *print(" A is greater")*

Output:

> *A is greater*

if else Statements

It also contains a Boolean expression. The if statement is followed by an optional else statement & if the expression results in FALSE, then else statement gets executed. It is also called alternative execution in which there are two possibilities of the condition determined in which any one of them will get executed.

> *if expression():*
> > *statement;*
> *else:*
> > *statement;*

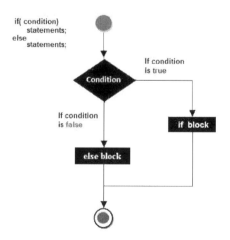

The if..else statement evaluates test expression and will execute body of if only when test condition is True . If the condition is False, body of else is executed. Indentation is used to separate the blocks. Python if..else statement syntax

Example:

> *a = 15*
> *b = 20*
>
> *if a > b:*
>
> > *print("A is greater")*
>
> *else:*
>
> > *print("B is greater")*

Output:

> *B is greater*

if elif else Statements

The elif is short for else if. It allows us to check for multiple expressions. If the condition for if is False , it checks the condition of the next elif block and so on. If all the conditions are False, body of else is executed.

> *if expression:*
>
> > *statement;*
>
> *elif expression:*
>
> > *statement;*
>
> *else:*
>
> > *statement;*

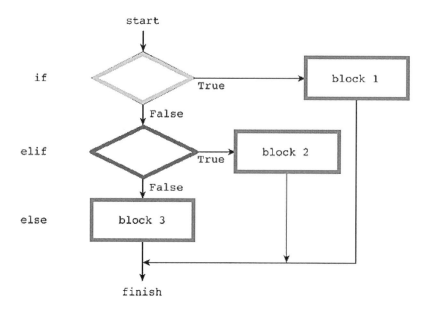

Only one block among the several if...elif...else blocks is executed according to the condition. The if block can have only one else block. But it can have multiple elif blocks. Python syntax for if elif else statements is as follows

Example:

> *a = 15*
> *b = 15*
>
> *if a > b:*
>   *print("A is greater")*
> *elif a == b:*
>   *print("A and B are equal")*
> *else:*
>   *print("B is greater")*

Output:
> *A and B are equal*

Nested if statements

We can implement if statement and or if-else statement inside another if or if – else statement. Here more than one if conditions are applied & there can be more than one if within else if. Python syntax of nested statement is as follows

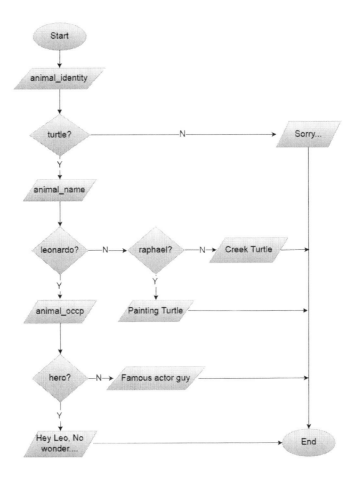

We can have a if...elif...else statement inside another if...elif...else statement. This is called nesting in computer programming. Any number of these statements can be nested inside one another. Indentation is the only way to _gure out the level of nesting. This can get confusing, so must be avoided if we can. Syntax for the nested if elif else is as follows:

if (test condition 1):

   # If test condition 1 is TRUE then it will check for test condition 2

   if (test condition 2):

      # If test condition 2 is TRUE then these statements will be executed

      Test condition 2 True statements

   else:

      # If test condition 2 is FALSE then these statements will be executed

      Test condition 2 False statements

else:

   # If test condition 1 is FALSE then these statements will be executed

   Test condition 1 False statements

Example :

```
num = float(input("Enter a number: "))
if num >= 0:
    if num == 0:
        print("Zero")
    else:
        print("Positive number")
else:
    print("Negative number")
```

Output :

```
Enter a number: 5
Positive number
```

Single Statement Condition

      If the block of executable statement of if – clause contains only a single line, programmers can write it on the same line as a header statement.

Example:

a = 15
if (a == 15): print("The value of a is 15")

Output:

The value of a is 15

4.2 LOOPS

A loop statement allows us to execute a statement or group of statements multiple times. In computer programming, a loop is a sequence of instruction s that is continually repeated until a certain condition is reached. Typically, a certain process is done, such as getting an item of data and changing it, and then some condition is checked such as whether a counter has reached a prescribed number. If it hasn't, the next instruction in the sequence is an instruction to return to the first instruction in the sequence and repeat the sequence. If the condition has been reached, the next instruction "falls through" to the next sequential instruction or branches outside the loop. A loop is a fundamental programming idea that is commonly used in writing programs.

An infinite loop is one that lacks a functioning exit routine . The result is that, the loop repeats continually until the operating system senses it and terminates the program, with an error or until some other event occurs, such as having the program automatically terminate after a certain duration of time.

Python programming language provides the following types of loops to handle looping requirements.

1. for loop
2. while loop
3. nested loop

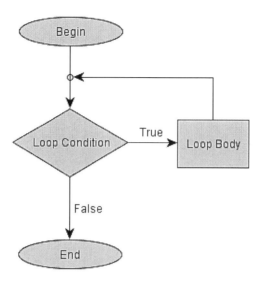

4.3 FOR LOOP STATEMENTS

A for loop executes its body multiple times. The for loop iterates over a sequence such as a list or string, and executes the body once for each element in the sequence. A for loop also de_nes a loop variable. On each iteration, the loop variable is assigned to the next sequence element. Here is an example of a for loop:

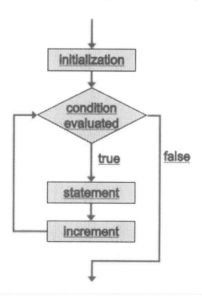

Syntax

for <variable> in <sequence>:

   <statements>

else:

   <statements>

Example:

for value in [1, 2, 6]:

   print value + 1

Output:

2

3

7

The for loop that is used to iterate over elements of a sequence, it is often used when you have a piece of code which you want to repeat "n" number of time. It works like this: " for all elements in a list, do this "

   computer_brands = ["Apple", "Asus", "Dell", "Samsung"]
   for brands in computer_brands:
   print brands

That reads, for every element that we assign the variable brands, in the list computer_brands, print out the variable brands

4.4 FOR LOOP EXAMPLE

```
for i in range(1,5):
print(i)
print("\n")
```

```
numbers = [1,10,20,30,40,50]
sum = 0
for num in numbers:
sum = sum + numbers
print sum
```

```
for i in range(1,10):
    print i
```

```
# Program to find the sum of all numbers stored in a list
# List of numbers
numbers = [6, 5, 3, 8, 4, 2, 5, 4, 11]
# variable to store the sum
sum = 0
# iterate over the list
for val in numbers:
    sum = sum+val
# Output: The sum is 48
print("The sum is", sum)

# Measure some strings:
words = ['cat', 'window', 'defenestrate']
for w in words:
    print(w, len(w))
```

4.5 WHILE LOOP STATEMENTS

In most computer programming languages, a while loop is a control flow statement that allows code to be executed repeatedly based on a given Boolean condition. The while loop can be thought of as a repeating if statement.

The while loop in Python is used to iterate over a block of code as long as the test expression or condition is true. We generally use this loop when we don't know beforehand, the number of times to iterate.

The while loop tells the computer to do something as long as the condition is met. Its construct consists of a block of code and a condition. The condition is evaluated and if the condition is true, the code within the block is executed. This repeats until the condition becomes false.

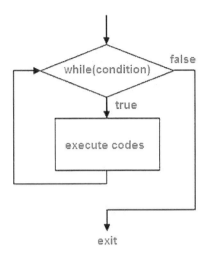

In while loop, test expression is checked first. The body of the loop is entered only if the test_expression evaluates to True. After one iteration, the test expression is checked again. This process continues until the test_expression evaluates to False.

In Python, the body of the while loop is determined through indentation. Body starts with indentation and the first unindented line marks the end. Python interprets any non-zero value as True. None and 0 are interpreted as False.

Syntax

while <TestExpression>:

    Body of while

Example:

a = 0

while a<10:

    a = a + 1

    print a

Output:

1 2 3 4 5 6 7 8 9

4.6 WHILE LOOP EXAMPLE

```
temperature = 115
while temperature > 122:
    print(temperature)
    temperature = temperature – 1


print('The coffee is cool enough")
```

```
# Program to add natural numbers
n = 10
sum = 0
i = 1

while i <= n:
  sum = sum + i
  i = i+1   # update counter

print("The sum is", sum)
```

```
while True:
    reply = raw_input('Enter text, type STOP to quit')
    print reply.lower()
    if reply == 'STOP' :
      break
```

while loop with else

Same as that of for loop, we can have an optional else block with while loop as well. The else part is executed if the condition in the while loop evaluates to False. The while loop can be terminated with a break statement. In such case, the else part is ignored. Hence, a while loop's else part runs if no break occurs and the condition is false. Here is an example to illustrate this.

Example:
 # Example to illustrate use of else statement with the while loop

counter = 0

while counter < 3:
  print("Inside loop")
  counter = counter + 1
else:
  print("Inside else")

Here, we use a counter variable to print the string Inside loop three times. On the fourth iteration, the condition in while becomes False. Hence, the else part is executed.

Output:
Inside loop
Inside loop
Inside loop
Inside else

4.7 THE NESTED LOOP

You can use one or more loop inside any another while, or for loop. The placing of one loop inside the body of another loop is called nesting. When you "nest" two loops, the outer loop takes control of the number of complete repetitions of the inner loop. While all types of loops may be nested, the most commonly nested loops are for loops.

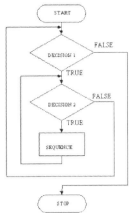

When working with nested loops, the outer loop changes only after the inner loop is completely finished or is interrupted.

Syntax

for [first iterating variable] in [outer loop]: # Outer loop

    [do something] # Optional

    for [second iterating variable] in [nested loop]: # Nested loop

      [do something]

Example:

for i in range(1,5):

    for j in range(i,5):

      print(i);

    print("\n")

Output:

1 1 1 1

2 2 2

3 3

4

4.8 LOOP CONTROL STATEMENTS

The Loop control statements change the execution from its normal sequence. When the execution leaves a scope, all automatic objects that were created in that scope are destroyed.

Python supports the following control sta tements.

1. break statement

2. continue statement

3. pass statement

1. *break statement:*

Terminates the loop statement and transfers execution to the statement immediately following the loop. The break statement only appears inside the body of a for or while loop. Executing a break statement immediately ends execution of the loop inside which it's declared. Here's an example of a break statement:

for i in range(1,10):

if i == 3:

   break

print i

The break keyword always appears on its own line, with no other expressions on the line. To execute a break statement, immediately end execution of the loop. Do not execute any more lines in the body of the loop. If the break statement is enclosed in a nested loop, only end execution of the innermost loop that contains the break statement.

Example:

 # i = 0, s = 'hello there'

for char in s:

   if char == ' ':

      break

   i += 1

Output:

h e l l o

2. *continue statement:*

Causes the loop to skip the remainder of its body and immediately retest its condition prior to reiterating. The continue statement is used to tell Python to skip the rest of the statements in the current loop block and to continue to the next iteration of the loop. Here's an example of a continue statement:

```
for i in range(1,10):
    if i == 3:
        continue
    print i
```

Like the break keyword, the continue keyword always appears on its own line, with no other expressions on the line. Note that in general, it is bad style to use continue because it is difficult to reason about.

The continue statement only appears inside the body of a for or while loop. Executing a continue statement immediately ends execution of the current iteration of the loop and skips to the next iteration as opposed to a break statement, which exits the loop completely.

Example:
```
for num in range(2, 10):
    if num % 2 == 0:
        print("Found an even number", num)
        continue
    print("Found a number", num)
```

Output:

Found an even number 2

Found a number 3

Found an even number 4

Found a number 5

Found an even number 6

Found a number 7

Found an even number 8

Found a number 9

3. pass statement:

The pass statement in Python is used when a statement is required syntactically but you do not want any command or code to execute.

Suppose we have a loop or a function that is not implemented yet, but we want to implement it in the future. They cannot have an empty body. The interpreter would complain.

So, we use the pass statement to construct a body that does nothing.
while True:

pass # Busy-wait for keyboard interrupt (Ctrl+C)

This is commonly used for creating minimal classes
class MyEmptyClass:
    pass

In Python programming, pass is a null statement. The difference between a comment and pass statement in Python is that, while the interpreter ignores a comment entirely, pass is not ignored. However, nothing happens when pass is executed. It results into no operation NOP. We generally use it as a placeholder.

Example:

```
#Generate a list of number
numbers = [ 1, 2, 4, 3, 6, 5, 7, 10, 9 ]
#Check for each number that belongs to the list
for number in numbers:
    #check if the number is even
    if number % 2 == 0:
        #if even, then pass ( No operation )
        pass
    else:
        #print the odd numbers
        print (number)
```

Output:
1 3 5 7 9

CHAPTER 5

PYTHON DATA STRUCTURES

Everything in Python that holds memory, in one or the other way, is considered as an Object and the type that the object belongs to is called as Data structure or Data type, in other words. An object is a part of memory with related data, which may be assigned or predefined, and is associated with a set operations.

So far, each value we have seen is a single datum, such as an integer, decimal number, or Boolean. Python also supports compound values, or data structures. A data structure contains multiple values. Examples include strings, lists, tuples, sets, and dictionaries.

Lists, strings and tuples are ordered sequences of objects. Unlike strings that contain only characters, list and tuples can contain any type of objects. Lists and tuples are like arrays. Tuples like strings are immutables. Lists are mutables so they can be extended or reduced at will. Sets are mutable unordered sequence of unique elements whereas frozensets are immutable sets.

Lists are enclosed in brackets:
fnam = [1, 2, "a"]

Tuples are enclosed in parentheses:
tick = (1, 2, "a")
Tuples are faster and consume less memory.

Dictionaries are built with curly brackets:
doc = {"a":1, "b":2}

Sets are made using the set() builtin function. More about the data structures here below:

Understanding data structures

We know three of the most common data types used in programming: numbers, strings and booleans. We assigned those data types to variables one-by-one, like so:
x = 3 # numbers
a = "gorillas" # strings
t = True # booleans

But what if we need something more complicated, like a product list? Assigning a variable for every item in the list would makes things very complicated:

```
prod_1 = "CPU"
prod_2 = "HDD"
prod_3 = "RAM"
```

5.1 PYTHON LISTS

Fortunately we don't have to do this. Instead, we have the list data type. An empty list is simply []

prod_list = []

When you are in the Python interpreter you can see what is inside a list by just typing the name of the list. For example:

>>> prod_list

[]

The interpreter shows us that the list is empty.

Now we can add items to prod_list. Try typing the following commands into the Python interpreter.

prod_list.append("CPU")
prod_list.append("HDD")
prod_list.append("RAM")

What is in the prod list? What happens when you append numbers or booleans to the list?

You can also assign a list with some items in it all in a single line, like this:

prod_list = ["milk", "cheese", "bread"]

To remove an item from the list we use remove():

prod_list.remove("milk")

Lists can easily be processed in a for loop. Have a look at this example which prints each item of the list in a new row:

for item in prod_list:
print(item)

And that's it! Python also makes it really easy to check if something is in a list or not:

```
        if "milk" in prod_list:
            print("Delicious!")


        if "eggs" not in prod_list:
        print("Well we can't have that!")
            prod_list.append("eggs")
```

Lists are the most common data structure in programming. There are lots of other things you can do with lists, and all languages have their own subtly different interpretation. But fundamentally they are all very similar.

5.2 PYTHON TUPLES

In Python, tuples are part of the standard language. This is a data structure very similar to the list data structure. The main difference being that tuple manipulation are faster than list because tuples are immutable.

So, Tuples are useful because they are faster than lists protect the data, which is immutable tuples can be used as keys on dictionaries

To create a tuple, place values within brackets:
```
>>> p = (1, 2, 3)
>>> p[0]
1
```

It is also possible to create a tuple without parentheses, by using commas:
```
>>> p = 1, 2
>>> p
(1, 2)
```

If you want to create a tuple with a single element, you must use the comma:
```
>>> singleton = (1, )
```

You can repeat a tuples by multiplying a tuple by a number:
```
>>> (1,) * 5
(1, 1, 1, 1, 1)
```

Note that you can concatenate tuples and use augmented assignement (*=, +=):

```
>>> s1 = (1, 0)
>>> s1 += (1,)
>>> s1
(1, 0, 1)
```

5.3 PYTHON DICTIONARIES

The other main data type is the dictionary. The dictionary allows you to associate one piece of data - key with another - value. The analogy comes from real-life dictionaries, where we associate a word the key with its meaning. It's a little harder to understand than a list, but Python makes them very easy to deal with.

You can create a dictionary with {}
laptop = {}

And you can add items to the dictionary like this:
laptop["model"] = "A good model works fine!"
laptop["price"] = "Cheap goes slow!"

The keys in this example are "model" and "price", and the values are the things that we assign to them. You can use any data type that won't change as a dictionary key. Check it out by using a number, a boolean value, and a list as keys in a dictionary. What does this say about strings?

As with lists, you can always see what is inside a dictionary:
>>> laptop
{'model': A good model works fine!', 'price': Cheap goes slow!'}

You can look up any entry in the dictionary by its key:
>>> laptop["model"]
'A good model works fine!'

If the key isn't found in the dictionary, a KeyError occurs:
>>> laptop["lenovo"]
Traceback (most recent call last):

File "<stdin>", line 1, in <module>
KeyError: 'lenovo'

For this reason, you can test whether a key is in the dictionary or not, by using the keyword in:
if "lenovo" in laptop:
print("Lenovo is one of the known laptop!")
print(laptop["lenovo"])
not in works as well, just like with lists.

You can delete from a dictionary as well. We don't really need to include an entry for price:
del laptop["price"]

What makes dictionaries so useful is that we can give meaning to the items within them. A list is just a bag of things, but a dictionary is a specific mapping of something to something else. By combining lists and dictionaries you can describe basically any data structure used in computing. Outside of Python, dictionaries are often called hash tables, hash maps or just maps.

5.4 PYTHON STRING

In short, strings are immutable sequence of characters. There are a lot of methods to ease manipulation and creation of strings as shown here below.

Single and double quotes are special characters. These are used to define strings. There are actually 3 ways to define a string using single, double or triple quotes:

text = 'The surface of the circle is 2 pi R = '
text = "The surface of the circle is 2 pi R = "
text = '''The surface of the circle is 2 pi R = '''

In fact the latest is generally written using triple double quotes:
text = """The surface of the circle is 2 pi R = """

Strings in double quotes work exactly the same as in single quotes but allow inserting single quote character inside them. The interest of the triple quotes (''' or """) is that you can specify multi-line strings. Moreover, single quotes and double quotes can be used freely within the triple quotes.

The mathematical operators + and * can be used to create new strings:

```
t = 'This is a test'
t2 = t+t
t3 = t*3
```

and comparison operators >, >=, ==, <=, < and != can be used to compare strings.

There are a few methods to check the type of alpha numeric characters present in a string: isdigit(), isalpha(), islower(), isupper(), istitle(), isspace(), str.isalnum():

```
>>> "44".isdigit()        # is the string made of digits o
True
>>> "44".isalpha()        # is the string made of alphabet
False
>>> "44".isalnum()        # is the string made of alphabet
True
>>> "Aa".isupper()        # is it made of upper cases only
False
>>> "aa".islower()        # or lower cases only ?
True
>>> "Aa".istitle()        # does the string start with a c
True
>>> text = "There are spaces but not only"
>>> text.isspace()        # is the string made of spaces on
False
```

You can count the occurrence of a character with count() or get the length of a string with len():

```
>>> mystr = "This is a string"
>>> mystr.count('i')
3
>>> len(mystr)
16
```

5.5 PYTHON SETS

This data type is used when the existence of an item is more important than its position. Simply, if we want to know whether 'Ravi' is present in a group of friends MitraSet, irrespective of its position in the group, we can use Python Sets. In other words, a Python set is an unordered list of unique items, but it is not of type list. A set can be created using Python built-in set() and providing a list of items as a parameter to it.

>>> MitraSet = set(['Rahim', 'Manisha', 'Jack'])

Here we have created the set named as MitraSet, which contains the list of friends. We have passed list object to set() function in the above example, but it is not the only way. You can also create it - using a valueless dictionary - as shown below:

>>> Bestfriend = set({'Manisha'})

The sets in Python logically resemble the sets in General Mathematics. You can find out Union and Intersection of two or more sets, as given below:

 # This operation returns common items, called as 'Intersection'
>>> MitraSet & Bestfriend
set(['Manisha'])

Same way, we can find out the difference between the sets, which will return unpaired values from both the sets.

 # This operation returns set of uncommon items
>>> MitraSet - Bestfriend
set(['Rahim', 'Jack'])

CHAPTER 6

VARIABLE AND DATA TYPES

6.1 PYTHON VARIABLES

A variable is a location in memory used to store some data value. They are given unique names to differentiate between different memory locations. The rules for writing a variable name are same as the rules for writing identifiers in Python.

We don't need to declare a variable before using it. In Python, we simply assign a value to a variable and it will exist. We don't even have to declare the type of the variable. This is handled internally according to the type of value we assign to the variable.

Python is a case-sensitive language. This means, variable and Variable are not the same. Always, name identifiers that make sense. While, c = 10 is valid. Writing count = 10 would make more sense and it would be easier to figure out what it does even when you look at your code after a long gap.

Multiple words can be separated using an underscore, this_is_a_long_variable. We can also use camel-case style of writing, i.e., capitalize every first letter of the word except the initial word without any spaces. For example: camelCaseExample.

Every language has rules for naming identifiers. The rules in python are the following. A valid identifier is a non-empty sequence of characters of any length with:

- The start character can be the underscore "_" or a capital or lower case letter.

- The letters following the start character can be anything which is permitted as a start character plus the digits.

- Identifiers are case-sensitive

- Python keywords are not allowed as identifier names

Variables in Python follow the standard nomenclature of an alphanumeric name beginning in a letter or underscore. Variable names are case sensitive. Variables do not need to be declared and their datatypes are inferred from the assignment statement.

6.2 VARIABLE ASSIGNMENT

We use the assignment operator (=) to assign values to a variable. Any type of value can be assigned to any valid variable.

a = 5
b = 3.2
c = "Hello"

Here, we have three assignment statements. 5 is an integer assigned to the variable *a*. Similarly, 3.2 is a floating point number and "Hello" is a string (sequence of characters) assigned to the variables *b* and *c* respectively.

Multiple assignments

In Python, multiple assignments can be made in a single statement as follows:

a, b, c = 5, 3.2, "Hello"

If we want to assign the same value to multiple variables at once, we can do this as:

x = y = z = "same"

This assigns the "same" string to all the three variables.

6.3 PYTHON KEYWORD

Python keyword is a special word that forms the vocabulary of the Python language. It is a reserved word that cannot be used as an identifier. They must be spelled exactly as they are written.

We cannot use a keyword as variable name, function name or any other identifier. They are used to define the syntax and structure of the Python language. In Python, keywords are case sensitive. There are 33 keywords in Python. This number can vary slightly in course of time. All the keywords except True, False and None are in lowercase and they must be written as it is. The list of all the keywords is given below.

Python keywords list

The following is a list of keywords for the Python programming language.

False	def	if	raise
None	del	import	return
True	elif	in	try

and	ele	is	while
as	except	lambda	with
assert	finally	nonlocal	yield
break	for not	class	from
or	continue	global	pass

Python is a dynamic language. It changes during time. The list of keywords may change in the future. To check the keywords you can write following code:

```
#!/usr/bin/python3
# keywords.py

import sys
import keyword

print("Python version: ", sys.version_info)
print("Python keywords: ", keyword.kwlist)
```

This script prints the version of Python and its actual keyword list.

```
$ ./keywords.py
Python version:  sys.version_info(major=3, minor=5, micro=2, release
level='final', serial=0)
Python keywords:  ['False', 'None', 'True', 'and', 'as', 'assert', 'break',
'class', 'continue', 'def', 'del', 'elif', 'else', 'except', 'finally', 'for', 'from',
'global', 'if', 'import', 'in', 'is', 'lambda', 'nonlocal', 'not', 'or', 'pass', 'raise',
'return', 'try', 'while', 'with', 'yield']
```

6.4 KEYWORDS EXPLAINED

print
print to console

while
controlling the flow of the program

for
iterate over items of a collection in order that they appear

break
interrupt the (loop) cycle, if needed

continue
used to interrupt the current cycle, without jumping out of the whole cycle. New cycle will begin.

if
used to determine, which statements are going to be executed.

elif
stands for else if.If the first test evaluates to False, then it continues with the next one

else
is optional. The statement after the else keyword is executed, unless the condition is True

is
tests for object identity

not
negates a boolean value

and
all conditions in a boolean expression must be met

or
at least one condition must be met.

import
import other modules into a Python script

as
if we want to give a module a different alias
from
for importing a specific variable, class or a function from a module

def
used to create a new user defined function

return
exits the function and returns a value

lambda
creates a new anonymous function

global
access variables defined outside functions

try
specifies exception handlers

except
catches the exception and executes codes

finally
is always executed in the end. Used to clean up resources.

raise
create a user defined exception

del
deletes objects

pass
does nothing

assert
used for debugging purposes

class
used to create new user defined objects

exec
executes Python code dynamically

yield

is used with generators

6.5 VARIABLE SCOPE

Most variables in Python are local in scope to their own function or class. For instance if you define a = 1 within a function, then a will be available within that entire function but will be undefined in the main program that calls the function. Variables defined within main program are accessible to the main program but not within the functions called by the main program. Global variable however can be declared with the global keyword in it.

```
a = 1
b = 2
def Sum():
  global a, b
  b = a + b
Sum()
print(b)
-> 3
```


6.6 DATA TYPES IN PYTHON

Every value in Python has a datatype. Since everything is an object in Python programming, data types are actually classes and variables are instance (object) of these classes. There are various data types in Python.

Type represents the kind of value and determines how the value can be used. All data values in Python are encapsulated in relevant object classes. Everything in Python is an object and every object has an identity, a type, and a value. Like another object-oriented language such as Java or C++, there are several data types which are built into Python. Extension modules which are written in C, Java, or other languages can define additional types.

To determine a variable's type in Python you can use the type() function. The value of some objects can be changed. Objects whose value can be changed are called mutable and objects whose value is unchangeable (once they are created) are called immutable. Here are the details of Python data types. Python has many native datatypes. Here are the important ones:

- Booleans are either True or False.

- Numbers can be integers like 1 and 2

- Numbers can be floats like 1.1 and 1.2

- Numbers can be fractions like ½ and 2/ 3

- Numbers can also be even complex numbers.

- Strings are sequences of Unicode characters.

- Bytes and byte arrays, e.g. a jpeg image file.

- Lists are ordered sequences of values.

- Tuples are ordered, immutable sequences of values.

- Sets are unordered bags of values.

- Dictionaries are unordered bags of key-value pairs.

6.7 NUMBERS

Any number you enter in Python will be interpreted as a number; you are not required to declare what kind of data type you are entering. Python will consider any number written without decimals as an integer (as in 138) and any number written with decimals as a float (as in 138.0).

Python supports four different numerical types –

- int - signed integers – They are often called just integers or ints, are positive or negative whole numbers with no decimal point.

- long - long integers – Also called longs, they are integers of unlimited size, written like integers and followed by an uppercase or lowercase L.

- Float numbers – Also called floats, they represent real numbers and are written with a decimal point dividing the integer and fractional parts. Floats may also be in scientific notation, with E or e indicating the power of 10 ($2.5e2 = 2.5 \times 10^2 = 250$).

- Complex numbers – are of the form a + bJ, where a and b are floats and J (or j) represents the square root of -1 (which is an imaginary number). The real part of the number is a, and the imaginary part is b. Complex numbers are not used much in Python programming.

Integers

Like in math, integers in computer programming are whole numbers that can be positive, negative, or 0 (..., -1, 0, 1, ...). An integer can also be known as an int. As with other programming languages, you should not use commas in numbers of four digits or more, so when you write 1,000 in your program, write it as 1000. We can print out an integer in a simple way like this:

print(-25)

Output

-25

Or, we can declare a variable, which in this case is essentially a symbol of the number we are using or manipulating, like so:

my_int = -25

print(my_int)

Output

-25

We can do math with integers in Python, too:

int_ans = 116 - 68

print(int_ans)

Output

48

Integers can be used in many ways within Python programs, and as you continue to learn more about the language you will have a lot of opportunities to work with integers and understand more about this data type.

Floating-Point Numbers

A floating-point number or a float is a real number, meaning that it can be either a rational or an irrational number. Because of this, floating-point numbers can be numbers that can contain a fractional part, such as 9.0 or -116.42. Simply speaking, for the purposes of thinking of a float in a Python program, it is a number that contains a decimal point.

Like we did with the integer, we can print out a floating-point number in a simple way like this:

print(17.3)

Output

17.3

We can also declare a variable that stands in for a float, like so:

my_flt = 17.3

print(my_flt)

Output

17.3

And, just like with integers, we can do math with floats in Python, too:

flt_ans = 564.0 + 365.24

print(flt_ans)

Output

929.24

With integers and floating-point numbers, it is important to keep in mind that 3 ≠ 3.0, as 3 refer to an integer while 3.0 refer to a float.

Here are some examples of numbers

int	long	float	complex
10	51924361L	0.0	3.14j
100	-0x19323L	15.20	45.j
-786	0122L	-21.9	9.322e-36j
080	0xDEFABCECBDAECBFBAEL	32.3+e18	.876j
-0490	535633629843L	-90.	-.6545+0J
-0x260	-052318172735L	-32.54e100	3e+26J
0x69	-4721885298529L	70.2-E12	4.53e-7j

Number Type Conversion

Python converts numbers internally in an expression containing mixed types to a common type for evaluation. But sometimes, you need to coerce a number explicitly from one type to another to satisfy the requirements of an operator or function parameter.

- Type int(x) to convert x to a plain integer.
- Type long(x) to convert x to a long integer.
- Type float(x) to convert x to a floating-point number.
- Type complex(x) to convert x to a complex number with real part x and imaginary part zero.
- Type complex(x, y) to convert x and y to a complex number with real part x and imaginary part y. x and y are numeric expressions

Mathematical Functions

Python includes following functions that perform mathematical calculations.

Function & Returns description
abs(x) Absolute value of x: the (positive) distance between x and zero.
ceil(x) The ceiling of x: the smallest integer not less than x
cmp(x, y) -1 if x < y, 0 if x == y, or 1 if x > y
exp(x) The exponential of x: e^x
fabs(x) The absolute value of x.
floor(x) The floor of x: the largest integer not greater than x
log(x) The natural logarithm of x, for x> 0
log10(x) The base-10 logarithm of x for x> 0.
max(x1, x2,...) The largest of its arguments: the value closest to positive infinity
min(x1, x2,...) The smallest of its arguments: the value closest to negative infinity
modf(x) The fractional and integer parts of x in a two-item tuple.
pow(x, y) The value of x**y.
round(x [,n]) x rounded to n digits from the decimal point.
sqrt(x) The square root of x for x > 0

Random Number Functions

Random numbers are used for games, simulations, testing, security, and privacy applications. Python includes following functions that are commonly used.

Function & Description
randrange ([start,] stop [,step]) A randomly selected element from range(start, stop, step)
random() Random float r, such as 0 is less than or equal to r and r is less than 1
seed([x]) Sets the integer starting value used in generating random numbers.
shuffle(lst) Randomizes the items of a list in place. Returns None.
uniform(x, y) Random float r, such as x is less than or equal to r and r is less than y

Trigonometric Functions

Python includes following functions that perform trigonometric calculations.

Function & Description
acos(x) Return the arc cosine of x, in radians.
asin(x) Return the arc sine of x, in radians.
atan(x) Return the arc tangent of x, in radians.
atan2(y, x) Return atan(y / x), in radians.
cos(x) Return the cosine of x radians.

hypot(x, y) Return the Euclidean norm, sqrt(x*x + y*y).
sin(x) Return the sine of x radians.
tan(x) Return the tangent of x radians.
degrees(x) Converts angle x from radians to degrees.
radians(x) Converts angle x from degrees to radians.

Booleans

Boolean values are the two constant objects False and True. They are used to represent truth values false or true.

In numeric contexts the argument behave like the integers 0 and 1, respectively. The built-in function bool() can be used to cast any value to a Boolean, if the value can be interpreted as a truth value. The y are written as False and True, respectively.

A string in Python can be tested for truth value. The return type will be in Boolean value i.e. True or False. Let us test using following example with a variable and string.

my_string = "Hello World"

```
my_string.isalnum()        #check if all char are numbers
my_string.isalpha()        #check if all char in the string are alphabetic
my_string.isdigit()        #test if string contains digits
my_string.istitle()        #test if string contains title words
my_string.isupper()        #test if string contains upper case
my_string.islower()        #test if string contains lower case
my_string.isspace()        #test if string contains spaces
my_string.endswith('d')    #test if string ends with a d
my_string.startswith('H')  #test if string starts with H
```

6.8 PYTHON OPERATORS

Operators are used to perform operations on values and variables. Operators can manipulate individual items and returns a result. The data items are referred as operands or arguments. Operators are either represented by keywords or special characters. For example, for identity operators we use keyword "is" and "is not".

Arithmetic Operators

Arithmetic Operators perform various arithmetic calculations like addition, subtraction, multiplication, division, %modulus, exponent, etc. There are various methods for arithmetic calculation in Python like you can use the eval function, declare variable & calculate, or call functions. For example, for arithmetic operators we will take simple example of addition where we will add two-digit 4+5=9

x= 4
y= 5
print x + y

The output of this code is "9."
Similarly, you can use other arithmetic operators like for multiplication(*), division (/), substraction (-), etc.

+ (addition)
Returns the sum of two expressions.

- (subtraction)
Returns the difference of two expressions.

* (multiplication)
Returns the product of two expressions.

** (power)
Returns the value of a numeric expression raised to a specified power.

/ (division)
Returns the quotient of two expressions.

// (floor division)
Returns the integral part of the quotient.

% (modulus)
Returns the decimal part (remainder) of the quotient.

Comparison Operators

These operators compare the values on either side of the operand and determine the relation between them. It is also referred as relational operators. Various comparison operators are (==, != , <>, >,<=, etc)

Example: For comparison operators we will compare the value of x to the value of y and print the result in true or false. Here in example, our value of x = 4 which is smaller than y = 5, so when we print the value as x>y, it actually compares the value of x to y and since it is not correct, it returns false.

x = 4
y = 5
print('x > y is',x>y)

The output of this code will be ('x > y is', False)
Likewise, you can try other comparison operators (x < y, x==y, x!=y, etc.)

== (equal)
Returns a Boolean stating whether two expressions are equal.

!= (not equal)
Returns a Boolean stating whether two expressions are not equal.

> (greater than)
Returns a Boolean stating whether one expression is greater than the other.

>= (greater than or equal)
Returns a Boolean stating whether one expression is greater than or equal the other.

< (less than)
Returns a Boolean stating whether one expression is less than the other.

<= (less than or equal)
Returns a Boolean stating whether one expression is less than or equal the other.

Python Assignment Operators

Python assignment operators are used for assigning the value of the right operand to the left operand. Various assignment operators used in Python are (+=, - = , *=, /= , etc.)

Example: Python assignment operators is simply to assign the value, for example

> *num1 = 4*
>
> *num2 = 5*
>
> *print ("Line 1 - Value of num1 : ", num1)*
>
> *print ("Line 2 - Value of num2 : ", num2)*

The output of this code will be

> *Line 1 - Value of num1: 4*
>
> *Line 2 - Value of num2: 5*

= (simple assignment)
Assigns a value to a variable(s).

+= (increment assignment)
Adds a value and the variable and assigns the result to that variable.

-= (decrement assignment)
Subtracts a value from the variable and assigns the result to that variable.

*= (multiplication assignment)
Multiplies the variable by a value and assigns the result to that variable.

/= (division assignment)
Divides the variable by a value and assigns the result to that variable.

**= (power assignment)
Raises the variable to a specified power and assigns the result to the variable.

%= (modulus assignment)
Computes the modulus of the variable and a value and assigns the result to that variable.

//= (floor division assignment)
Floor divides the variable by a value and assigns the result to that variable.

Compound assignment operator

We can also use a compound assignment operator, where you can add, subtract, multiply right operand to left and assign addition (or any other arithmetic function) to the left operand.

Example:

num1 = 4

num2 = 5

res = num1 + num2

res += num1

print ("Line 1 - Result of + is ", res)

The output of this code will be

Line 1 - Result of + is 13

Logical Operators

Logical operators in Python are used for conditional statements are true or false. Logical operators in Python are AND, OR and NOT. For logical operators following condition are applied.

- AND – It returns TRUE if both the operands are true
- OR - It returns TRUE if either of the operand is true
- For NOT operator- returns TRUE if operand is false

Example: Here in example we get true or false based on the value of a and b

a = True

b = False

print('a and b is',a and b)

print('a or b is',a or b)

print('not a is',not a)

The output of this code will be

a and b is, False

a or b is, True

not a is, False

and

Returns the first operand that evaluates to *False* or the last one if all are *True*.

_or_

Returns the first operand that evaluates to *True* or the last one if all are *False*.

not

Returns a boolean that is the reverse of the logical state of an expression.

Membership Operators

These operators test for membership in a sequence such as lists, strings or tuples. There are two membership operators that are used in Python. (in, not in). It gives the result based on the variable present in specified sequence or string.

Example: For example here we check whether the value of x=4 and value of y=8 is available in list or not, by using in and not in operators.

```
x = 4
y = 8
list = [1, 2, 3, 4, 5 ];

if ( x in list ):
   print "Line 1 - x is available in the given list"
else:
   print "Line 1 - x is not available in the given list"

if ( y not in list ):
   print "Line 2 - y is not available in the given list"
else:
   print "Line 2 - y is available in the given list"
```

The output of this code is

Line 1 - x is available in the given list

Line 2 - y is not available in the given list

Identity Operators

To compare the memory location of two objects, Identity Operators are used. The two identify operators used in Python are (is, is not).

- is: It returns true if two variables point the same object and false otherwise
- is not: It returns false if two variables point the same object and true otherwise

Example:
x = 20
y = 20

if (x is y):
        print "x & y SAME identity"

y=30

if (x is not y):
        print "x & y have DIFFERENT identity"

The output of this code will be
        x & y SAME identity
        x & y have DIFFERENT identity

Callables Operators

* (tuple packing)
Packs the consecutive function positional arguments into a tuple.

** (dictionary packing)
Packs the consecutive function keyword arguments into a dictionary.

* (tuple unpacking)
Unpacks the contents of a tuple into the function call.

** (dictionary unpacking)
Unpacks the contents of a dictionary into the function call.

@ (decorator)
Returns a callable wrapped by another callable.

() (call operator)
Calls a callable object with specified arguments.

lambda
Returns an anonymous function.

Bitwise Operators

& (bitwise AND)
Returns the result of bitwise AND of two integers.

| (bitwise OR)
Returns the result of bitwise OR of two integers.

^ (bitwise XOR)
Returns the result of bitwise XOR of two integers.

<< (left shift)
Shifts the bits of the first operand left by the specified number of bits.

>> (right shift)
Shifts the bits of the first operand right by the specified number of bits.

~ (bitwise complement)
Sets the 1 bits to 0 and 1 to 0 and then adds 1.

Bitwise Assignment Operators

&= (bitwise AND assignment)
Performs bitwise AND and assigns value to the left operand.

|= (bitwise OR assignment)
Performs bitwise OR and assigns value to the left operand.

^= (bitwise XOR assignment)
Performs bitwise XOR and assigns value to the left operand.

<<= (bitwise right shift assignment)
Performs bitwise left shift and assigns value to the left operand.

>>= (bitwise left shift assignment)
Performs bitwise right shift and assigns value to the left operand.

Misc

; (statement separator)
Separates two statements.

(line continuation)
Breaks the line of code allowing for the next line continuation.

. (attribute access)
Gives access to an object's attribute.

String and Sequence Operators
+ (concatenation)
Returns a concatenation of two sequences.

* (multiple concatenation)
Returns a sequence self-concatenated specified amount of times.

% (string formatting operator)
Formats the string according to the specified format.

Sequence Assignment Operators

+= (concatenation assignment)

Concatenates the sequence with the right operand and assigns the result to that sequence.

*= (multiple concatenation assignment)
Multiple concatenates the sequence and assigns the result to that sequence.

6.9 OPERATOR PRECEDENCE

The operator precedence determines which operators need to be evaluated first. To avoid ambiguity in values, precedence operators are necessary. Just like in normal multiplication method, multiplication has a higher precedence than addition. For example in 3+ 4*5, the answer is 23, to change the order of precedence we use a square bracket (3+4)*5, now the answer is 35. Precedence operator used in Python are (unary + - ~, **, * / %, + - , &) etc.

Example:
   v = 4
   w = 5

```
x = 8
y = 2
z = 0
z = (v+w) * x / y;
print "Value of (v+w) * x/ y is ",  z
```

The output of this result is

Value of (v+w) * x/ y is 36

CHAPTER 7

PYTHON FUNCTIONS

7.1 WHAT ARE FUNCTIONS

Functions are a convenient way to divide your code into useful blocks, allowing us to order our code, make it more readable, reuse it and save some time. Also functions are a key way to define interfaces so programmers can share their code.

Functions are common to all programming languages, and it can be defined as a block of re-usable code to perform specific tasks. But defining functions in Python means knowing both types first: built-in and user-defined. Built-in functions are usually a part of Python packages and libraries, whereas user-defined functions are written by the developers to meet certain requirements. In Python, all functions are treated as objects, so it is more flexible compared to other high-level languages.

Functions are a construct to structure programs. They are known in most programming languages, sometimes also called subroutines or procedures. Functions are used to utilize code in more than one place in a program. The only way without functions to reuse code consists in copying the code. A function in Python is defined by a def statement. The general syntax looks like this:

```
def function-name(Parameter list):
    statements, i.e. the function body
```

The parameter list consists of none or more parameters. Parameters are called arguments, if the function is called. The function body consists of indented statements. The function body gets executed every time the function is called. Parameter can be mandatory or optional. The optional parameters zero or more must follow the mandatory parameters.

Function bodies can contain a return statement. It can be anywhere in the function body. This statement ends the execution of the function call and "returns" the result, i.e. the value of the expression following the return keyword, to the caller. If there is no return statement in the function code, the function ends, when the control flow reaches the end of the function body.

7.2 USER-DEFINED FUNCTIONS IN PYTHON

In general, developers can write user-defined functions or it can be borrowed as a third-party library. This also means your own user-defined functions can also be a third-party library for other users. User-defined functions have certain advantages depending when and how they are used. Let's have a look at the following points.

- User-defined functions are reusable code blocks; they only need to be written once, then they can be used multiple times. They can even be used in other applications, too.

- These functions are very useful, from writing common utilities to specific business logic. These functions can also be modified per requirement.

- The code is usually well organized, easy to maintain, and developer-friendly. Which means it can support the modular design approach.

- As user-defined functions can be written independently, the tasks of a project can be distributed for rapid application development.

- A well-defined and thoughtfully written user-defined function can ease the application development process.

7.3 DIFFERENT FUNCTION ARGUMENTS IN PYTHON.

Function arguments in Python

In Python, user-defined functions can take four different types of arguments. The argument types and their meanings, however, are pre-defined and can't be changed. But a developer can, instead, follow these pre-defined rules to make their own custom functions. The following are the four types of arguments and their rules.

1. Default arguments:

Python has a different way of representing syntax and default values for function arguments. Default values indicate that the function argument will take that value if no argument value is passed during function call. The default value is assigned by using assignment = operator. Below is a typical syntax for default argument. Here, msg parameter has a default value Hello!.

Function definition
def defaultArg(name, msg = "Hello!"):

Function call
defaultArg(name)

Example:

def defArgFunc(empname, emprole = "Manager"):
  print ("Emp Name: ", empname)
  print ("Emp Role ", emprole)
  return;
print("Using default value")

defArgFunc(empname="Nick")
*print("**********************")*
print("Overwriting default value")

defArgFunc(empname="Tom",emprole = "CEO")

2. Required arguments:

Required arguments are the mandatory arguments of a function. These argument values must be passed in correct number and order during function call. Below is a typical syntax for a required argument function.

Function definition
def requiredArg (str,num):

Function call
requiredArg ("Hello",12)

Example:

def reqArgFunc(empname):

  print ("Emp Name: ", empname)

  return;

print("Not passing required arg value")

reqArgFunc()

print("Now passing required arg value"*)*

reqArgFunc("Hello"*)*

3. Keyword arguments:

Keyword arguments are relevant for Python function calls. The keywords are mentioned during the function call along with their corresponding values. These keywords are mapped with the function arguments so the function can easily identify the corresponding values even if the order is not maintained during the function call. The following is the syntax for keyword arguments.

Function definition
def keywordArg(name, role)*:*

Function call
keywordArg(name = "Ravi", role = "Manager")

or
keywordArg(role = "Manager", name = "Ravi")

Example:

def keyArgFunc(empname, emprole):

  print *(*"Emp Name: "*, empname)*

  print *(*"Emp Role: "*, emprole)*

  return*;*

print("Calling in proper sequence"*)*

*keyArgFunc(empname = *"Nick"*,emprole = *"Manager" *)*

print("Calling in opposite sequence"*)*

*keyArgFunc(emprole = *"Manager"*,empname = *"Nick"*)*

4. Variable number of arguments:

This is very useful when we do not know the exact number of arguments that will be passed to a function. Or we can have a design where any number of arguments can be passed based on the requirement. Below is the syntax for this type of function call.

Function definition
def varlengthArgs(*varargs):

Function call
varlengthArgs(30,40,50,60)

Example:

def varLenArgFunc(*varvallist):

  print ("The Output is: ")

  for varval in varvallist:

   print (varval)

  return;

 print("Calling with single value")

 varLenArgFunc(55)

 print("Calling with multiple values")

 varLenArgFunc(50,60,70,80)

7.4 WRITING USER-DEFI[NED FUNCTIONS IN PYTHON

These are the basic steps in writing user-defined functions in Python. For additional functionalities, we need to incorporate more steps as needed.

- **Step 1:** Declare the function with the keyword def followed by the function name.

- **Step 2:** Write the arguments inside the opening and closing parentheses of the function, and end the declaration with a colon.

- **Step 3:** Add the program statements to be executed.

- **Step 4:** End the function with/without return statement.

 def userDefFunction (arg1, arg2, arg3 ...):

  program statement1

  program statement3

program *statement3*

....

return;

7.5 FUNCTION SCOPE

Python does support global variables without you having to explicitly express that they are global variables. It's much easier just to show rather than explain:

Example
```
def someFunction():
a = 10
someFunction()
print (a)
```

This will cause an error because our variable, a, is in the local scope of someFunction. So, when we try to print a, Python will bite and say a isn't defined. Technically, it is defined, but just not in the global scope. Now, let's look at an example that works.

Example
```
a = 10
def someFunction():
print (a)
someFunction()
```

In this example, we defined a in the global scope. This means that we can call it or edit it from anywhere, including inside functions. However, you cannot declare a variable inside a function, local scope, to be used outside in a global scope.

CHAPTER 8

PYTHON PRACTICAL PROGRAMS

8.1 CALCULATE THE AVERAGE OF NUMBERS IN A GIVEN LIST

Here is source code of the Python Program to Calculate the Average of Numbers in a Given List. The program output is also shown below.

```
n=int(input("Enter the number of elements to be inserted: "))
a=[]
for i in range(0,n):
    elem=int(input("Enter element: "))
    a.append(elem)
avg=sum(a)/n
print("Average of elements in the list",round(avg,2))
```

Program Explanation

- User must first enter the number of elements which is stored in the variable.
- The value of I ranges from 0 to the number of elements and is incremented each time after the body of the loop is executed.
- Then, the element that the user enters is stored in the variable elem.
- a.append(elem) appends the element to the list.
- Now the value of i is incremented to 2.
- The new value entered by the user for the next loop iteration is now stored in elem which is appended to the list.
- The loop runs till the value of i reaches n.
- sum(a) gives the total sum of all the elements in the list and dividing it by the total number of elements gives the average of elements in the list.
- round(avg,2) rounds the average upto 2 decimal places.
- Then the average is printed after rounding.

Runtime Test Cases

Case 1:
Enter the number of elements to be inserted: 3
Enter element: 23
Enter element: 45
Enter element: 56
Average of elements in the list 41.33

Case 2:
Enter the number of elements to be inserted: 5
Enter element: 12
Enter element: 24
Enter element: 33
Enter element: 25
Enter element: 18
Average of elements in the list 22.4

8.2 PYTHON PROGRAM TO REVERSE A GIVEN NUMBER

This is a Python Program to reverse a given number. The program takes a number and reverses it.

Problem Solution

- Take the value of the integer and store in a variable.
- Using a while loop, get each digit of the number and store the reversed number in another variable.
- Print the reverse of the number.
- Exit.

Program Source Code
Here is the source code of the Python Program to reverse a given number.

```
n=int(input("Enter number: "))
rev=0
```

```
while(n>0):
    dig=n%10
    rev=rev*10+dig
    n=n//10
print("Reverse of the number:",rev)
```

Program Explanation

- User must first enter the value and store it in a variable n.

- The while loop is used and the last digit of the number is obtained by using the modulus operator.

- The last digit is then stored at the one's place, second last at the ten's place and so on.

- The last digit is then removed by truly dividing the number with 10.

- This loop terminates when the value of the number is 0.

- The reverse of the number is then printed.

Runtime Test Cases

Case 1:
Enter number: 124
Reverse of the number: 421

Case 2:
Enter number: 4538
Reverse of the number: 8354

8.3 CHECK WHETHER A NUMBER IS POSITIVE OR NEGATIVE.

This is a Python Program to check whether a number is positive or negative. The program takes a number and checks whether it is positive or negative.

Problem Solution

- Take the value of the integer and store in a variable.

- Use an if statement to determine whether the number is positive or negative.

- Exit.

Program Source Code

Here is the source code of the Python Program to check whether a number is positive or negative. The program output is also shown below.

```
n=int(input("Enter number: "))
if(n>0):
    print("Number is positive")
else:
    print("Number is negative")
```

Program Explanation

- User must first enter the value and store it in a variable.

- Use an if statement to make a decision.

- If the value of the number is greater than 0, "Number is positive" is printed.

- If the value of the number if lesser than 0, "Number is negative" is negative.

Runtime Test Cases

```
Case 1:
Enter number: 45
Number is positive

Case 2:
Enter number: -30
Number is negative
```

8.4 TAKE IN THE MARKS OF 5 SUBJECTS AND DISPLAY THE GRADE

This is a Python Program to take in the marks of 5 subjects and display the grade. The program takes in the marks of 5 subjects and displays the grade.

Problem Solution

- Take in the marks of 5 subjects from the user and store it in different variables.

- Find the average of the marks.

- Use an else condition to decide the grade based on the average of the marks.

- Exit.

Program Source Code
Here is source code of the Python Program to take in the marks of 5 subjects and display the grade. The program output is also shown below.

```
sub1=int(input("Enter marks of the first subject: "))
sub2=int(input("Enter marks of the second subject: "))
sub3=int(input("Enter marks of the third subject: "))
sub4=int(input("Enter marks of the fourth subject: "))
sub5=int(input("Enter marks of the fifth subject: "))
avg=(sub1+sub2+sub3+sub4+sub4)/5
if(avg>=90):
    print("Grade: A")
elif(avg>=80&avg<90):
    print("Grade: B")
elif(avg>=70&avg<80):
    print("Grade: C")
elif(avg>=60&avg<70):
```

```
    print("Grade: D")
  else:
    print("Grade: F")
```

Program Explanation

- User must enter 5 different values and store it in separate variables.

- Then sum up all the five marks and divide by 5 to find the average of the marks.

- If the average is greater than 90, "Grade: A" is printed.

- If the average is in between 80 and 90, "Grade: B" is printed.

- If the average is in between 70 and 80, "Grade: C" is printed.

- If the average is in between 60 and 70, "Grade: D" is printed.

- If the average is anything below 60, "Grade: F" is printed.

Runtime Test Cases

```
Case 1:
Enter marks of the first subject: 85
Enter marks of the second subject: 95
Enter marks of the third subject: 99
Enter marks of the fourth subject: 93
Enter marks of the fifth subject: 100
Grade: A

Case 2:
Enter marks of the first subject: 81
Enter marks of the second subject: 72
Enter marks of the third subject: 94
Enter marks of the fourth subject: 85
Enter marks of the fifth subject: 80
Grade: B
```

8.5 READ TWO NUMBERS, PRINT THEIR QUOTIENT AND REMAINDER

This is a Python Program to read two numbers and print their quotient and remainder. The program takes two numbers and prints the quotient and remainder.

Problem Solution

- Take in the first and second number and store it in separate variables.

- Then obtain the quotient using division and the remainder using modulus operator.

- Exit.

Program Source Code

Here is the source code of the Python Program to read two numbers and print their quotient and remainder. The program output is also shown below.

```
a=int(input("Enter the first number: "))
b=int(input("Enter the second number: "))
quotient=a//b
remainder=a%b
print("Quotient is:",quotient)
print("Remainder is:",remainder)
```

Program Explanation

- User must enter the first and second number .

- The quotient is obtained using true division (// operator).

- The modulus operator gives remainder when a is divided by b.

Runtime Test Cases

Case 1:
Enter the first number: 15

Enter the second number: 7
Quotient is: 2
Remainder is: 1

Case 2:
Enter the first number: 125
Enter the second number: 7
Quotient is: 17
Remainder is: 6

8.6 PRINT ODD NUMBERS WITHIN A GIVEN RANGE

This is a Python Program to print odd numbers within a given range. The program takes the upper and lower limit and prints all odd numbers within a given range.

Problem Solution

- Take in the upper range limit and the lower range limit and store it in separate variables.

- Use a for-loop ranging from the lower range to the upper range limit.

- Then use an if statement if check whether the number is odd or not and print the number.

- Exit.

Program Source Code

Here is the source code of the Python Program to print odd numbers within a given range. The program output is also shown below.

```
lower=int(input("Enter the lower limit for the range:"))

upper=int(input("Enter the upper limit for the range:"))

for i in range(lower,upper+1):

    if(i%2!=0):

        print(i)
```

Program Explanation

- User must enter the upper range limit and the lower range limit.

- The for loop ranges from the lower range limit to the upper range limit.

- The expression within the if-statement checks if the remainder obtained when the number divided by 2 is one or not (using the % operator).

- If the remainder isn't equal to 0, the number is odd and hence the number is printed.

Runtime Test Cases

Case 1:
Enter the lower limit for the range:1
Enter the upper limit for the range:16
1
3
5
7
9
11
13
15

Case 2:
Enter the lower limit for the range:150
Enter the upper limit for the range:180
151
153
155
157
159
161
163
165
167
169
171
173

175
177
179

8.7 COMPUTE SIMPLE INTEREST GIVEN ALL THE REQUIRED VALUES

This is a Python Program to compute simple interest given all the required values. The program computes simple interest given the principle amount, rate and time.

Problem Solution

- Take in the values for principle amount, rate and time.
- Using the formula, compute the simple interest.
- Print the value for the computed interest.
- Exit.

Program Source Code

Here is source code of the Python Program to compute simple interest given all the required values. The program output is also shown below.

```
principle=float(input("Enter the principle amount:"))
time=int(input("Enter the time(years):"))
rate=float(input("Enter the rate:"))
simple_interest=(principle*time*rate)/100
print("The simple interest is:",simple_interest)
```

Program Explanation

- User must enter the values for the principle amount, rate and time.
- The formula: (amount*time*rate)/100 is used to compute simple interest.
- The simple interest is later printed.

Runtime Test Cases

> *Case 1:*
> *Enter the principle amount:200*
> *Enter the time(years):5*
> *Enter the rate:5.0*
> *The simple interest is: 50.0*
>
> *Case 2:*
> *Enter the principle amount:70000*
> *Enter the time(years):1*
> *Enter the rate:4.0*
> *The simple interest is: 2800.0*

8.8 CHECK IF A NUMBER IS A PRIME NUMBER

This is a Python Program to check if a number is a prime number. The program takes in a number and checks if it is a prime number.

Problem Solution

- Take in the number to be checked and store it in a variable.

- Initialize the count variable to 0.

- Let the for loop range from 2 to half of the number excluding 1 and the number itself.

- Then find the number of divisors using the if statement and increment the count variable each time.

- If the number of divisors is lesser than or equal to 0, the number is prime.

- Print the final result.

- Exit.

Program Source Code
Here is source code of the Python Program to check if a number is a prime number. The program output is also shown below.

```
a=int(input("Enter number: "))
k=0
for i in range(2,a//2):
    if(a%i==0):
        k=k+1
if(k<=0):
    print("Number is prime")
else:
    print("Number isn't prime")
```

Program Explanation

- User must enter the number to be checked and store it in a different variable.
- The count variable is first initialized to 0.
- The for loop ranges from 2 to the half of the number so 1 and the number itself aren't counted as divisors.
- The if statement then checks for the divisors of the number if the remainder is equal to 0.
- The count variable counts the number of divisors and if the count is lesser or equal to 0, the number is a prime number.
- If the count is greater than 0, the number isn't prime.
- The final result is printed.

Runtime Test Cases

Case 1:
Enter number: 7
Number is prime

Case 2:
Enter number: 35
Number isn't prime

8.8 PUT EVEN AND ODD ELEMENTS INTO TWO DIFFERENT LISTS

This is a Python Program to put the even and odd elements in a list into two different lists. The program takes a list and puts the even and odd elements in it into two separate lists.

Problem Solution

- Take in the number of elements and store it in a variable.
- Take in the elements of the list one by one.
- Use a for loop to traverse through the elements of the list and an if statement to check if the element is even or odd.
- If the element is even, append it to a separate list and if it is odd, append it to a different one.
- Display the elements in both the lists.
- Exit.

Program/Source Code
Here is source code of the Python Program to put the even and odd elements in a list into two different lists. The program output is also shown below.

```
a=[]
n=int(input("Enter number of elements:"))
for i in range(1,n+1):
    b=int(input("Enter element:"))
    a.append(b)
even=[]
odd=[]
for j in a:
    if(j%2==0):
        even.append(j)
    else:
```

odd.append(j)

print("The even list",even)

print("The odd list",odd)

Program Explanation

- User must enter the number of elements and store it in a variable.

- User must then enter the elements of the list one by one using a for loop and store it in a list.

- Another for loop is used to traverse through the elements of the list.

- The if statement checks if the element is even or odd and appends them to separate lists.

- Both the lists are printed.

Runtime Test Cases

Case 1:
Enter number of elements:5
Enter element:67
Enter element:43
Enter element:44
Enter element:22
Enter element:455
The even list [44, 22]
The odd list [67, 43, 455]

Case 2:
Enter number of elements:3
Enter element:23
Enter element:44
Enter element:99
The even list [44]
The odd list [23, 99]

8.9 COUNT THE NUMBER OF VOWELS IN A STRING

This is a Python Program to count the number of vowels in a string. The program takes a string and counts the number of vowels in a string.

Problem Solution

- Take a string from the user and store it in a variable.
- Initialize a count variable to 0.
- Use a for loop to traverse through the characters in the string.
- Use an if statement to check if the character is a vowel or not and increment the count variable if it is a vowel.
- Print the total number of vowels in the string.
- Exit.

Program Source Code

Here is source code of the Python Program to remove the nth index character from a non-empty string. The program output is also shown below.

```
string=raw_input("Enter string:")
vowels=0
for i in string:
    if(i=='a' or i=='e' or i=='i' or i=='o' or i=='u' or i=='A' or i=='E' or i=='I' or i=='O' or i=='U'):
        vowels=vowels+1
print("Number of vowels are:")
print(vowels)
```

Program Explanation

- User must enter a string and store it in a variable.
- The count variable is initialized to zero.

- The for loop is used to traverse through the characters in the string.

- An if statement checks if the character is a vowel or not.

- The count is incremented each time a vowel is encountered.

- The total count of vowels in the string is printed.

Runtime Test Cases

Case 1:
Enter string:Hello world
Number of vowels are:
3

Case 2:
Enter string:WELCOME
Number of vowels are:
3

8.10 CHECK IF A GIVEN KEY EXISTS IN A DICTIONARY OR NOT

This is a Python Program to check if a given key exists in a dictionary or not. The program takes a dictionary and checks if a given key exists in a dictionary or not.

Problem Solution

- Declare and initialize a dictionary to have some key-value pairs.

- Take a key from the user and store it in a variable.

- Using an if statement and the in operator, check if the key is present in the dictionary using the dictionary.keys() method.

- If it is present, print the value of the key.

- If it isn't present, display that the key isn't present in the dictionary.

- Exit.

Program Source Code

Here is source code of the Python Program to check if a given key exists in a dictionary or not. The program output is also shown below.

```
d={'A':1,'B':2,'C':3}
key=raw_input("Enter key to check:")
if key in d.keys():
    print("Key is present and value of the key is:")
    print(d[key])
else:
    print("Key isn't present!")
```

Program Explanation

- User must enter the key to be checked and store it in a variable.
- An if statement and the in operator is used check if the key is present in the list containing the keys of the dictionary.
- If it is present, the value of the key is printed.
- If it isn't present, "Key isn't present!" is printed.
- Exit.

Runtime Test Cases

Case 1:
Enter key to check:A
Key is present and value of the key is:
1

Case 2:
Enter key to check:F
Key isn't present!

8.11 CHECK COMMON LETTERS IN TWO INPUT STRINGS

This is a Python Program to check common letters in the two input strings. The program takes two strings and checks common letters in both the strings.

Problem Solution

- Enter two input strings and store it in separate variables.
- Convert both of the strings into sets and find the common letters between both the sets.
- Store the common letters in a list.
- Use a for loop to print the letters of the list.
- Exit.

Program/Source Code
Here is source code of the Python Program to check common letters in the two input strings. The program output is also shown below.

```
s1=raw_input("Enter first string:")
s2=raw_input("Enter second string:")
a=list(set(s1)&set(s2))
print("The common letters are:")
for i in a:
    print(i)
```

Program Explanation

- User must enter two input strings and store it in separate variables.
- Both of the strings are converted into sets and the common letters between both the sets are found using the '&' operator.
- These common letters are stored in a list.
- A for loop is used to print the letters of the list.

Runtime Test Cases

Case 1:
Enter first string:Hello
Enter second string:How are you
The common letters are:
H
e
o

Case 2:
Enter first string:Test string
Enter second string:checking
The common letters are:
i
e
g
n

ABOUT THE AUTHOR

Firoz Kayum Kajrekar received his B.Sc degree from S P K Mahavidyalaya, Sawantwadi under Mumbai University, India, and completed Master Computer Application – MCA from SIBER under Shivaji University, Kolhapur, India and was awarded with PhD degree in Computer Science and Engineering from Singhania University, Rajasthan, India. Have experience of more than fifteen years in computer field. Worked as a Senior Lecturer in S P K College, Sawantwadi, India and also worked as Senior Lecturer in Caledonian College of Engineering, Al Hail, Oman and also as Lecturer in Higher College of Technology in Muscat, Oman. Working as Assistant Professor in SPK Mahavidyalaya, in Computer Science and Information Technology department.

Printed in Great Britain
by Amazon